Danite's Group Bible Study Series & Otakada.Org Publishing

Responses To The Word

Revised Edition 2019

Raphael Awoseyin

Table of Contents

Danite's Group Bible Study Series & Otakada.Org Publishing 1
Responses To The Word 1
Revised Edition 2019 1
Raphael Awoseyin 1
Introduction 5
About the Author 7
About the Publisher – Otakada.org 8
This Edition 9
Study 1 - Consider What You Hear! 10
Main Text: Mark 4:1-29 10
Discussion Questions: 11
Key Learning Points: 11
Prayer: 12
Study 2 - Nicodemus 13
Main Texts: John 3:1-15; 19:38-42 13
Discussion Questions: 15
Key Learning Points: 15
Prayer: 15
Study 3 - Admirers and Agreers 17
Main Texts: Mark 12:18-34; Luke 11:14-28 17
Discussion Questions: 18
Key Learning Points: 19
Prayer: 19
Study 4 - Jairus 20
Main Texts: Mark 5:21-43 20
Questions 21
Key Learning Points: 22
Prayer: 22

Study 5 - The centurion's servant 24
Main Text: Luke 7:1-10, Matthew 8:5-13 24
Discussion Questions: 25
Key Learning Points: 26
Prayer: 26

Study 6 - Levels of Faith 27
Main Text: Mark 5:22-43, Matthew 8:5-13 27
Key Learning Points: 28
Prayer: 29

Study 7 - The Pentecost Crowd 30
Main Text: Acts 2:1-41 30
Key Learning Points: 31
Prayer: 32

Study 8 – Apostle Paul 33
Main Text: Galatians 2:11-24; 2 Corinthians 11:23-33 33
Key Learning Points: 34
Prayer: 35

Study 9 - Thessalonians and Bereans 36
Main Text: Acts 17:1-15 36
Key Learning Points: 38
Prayer: 38

Study 10 - The Ephesians 39
Main Text: Acts 19:1-41 39
Key Learning Points: 41
Prayer: 41

Study 11 – Governor Felix 42
Main Text: Acts 24:1-27 42
Key Learning Points: 43
Prayer: 44

Study 12 - Festus and Agrippa 45
Main Texts: Acts 26:1-32 45

Key Learning Points: 47
Prayer: 47

Introduction

Throughout the world, Christian groups meet regularly for bible studies, often within tight time constraints. Such meetings include what we call the Sunday School – typically before a Church worship service. A major challenge of these fellowships is the need to have a study that can be completed within the tight schedule, and yet leave participants with learning that they can apply to their daily lives. The Danite Group Bible Study (DGBS) series is a response to this challenge.

The series have two objectives: First, they must lead to practical applications of bible principles to the lives of participants and to their environment. Secondly, each study material must be of the right length for a meaningful one-hour group study.

Each edition of DBGS is based on a theme intended for a quarter of a year (3 months) and comprises twelve studies. The intent is that the group takes a one-hour study each week on the quarterly theme.

To get the most out of each study, it is important that the study be participatory. Reading of the main texts should be shared among participants, after which all should read the key verse together. The paragraphs in the study, written in a teaching style, are read by individuals nominated by the leader while the questions that follow stimulate discussion. At the end of each study, a few bullet-point lessons are suggested. The study leaders should highlight these points as well as additional learning that may emerge from the discussions.

While the materials are aimed at group bible studies, individuals should also find them helpful in personal studies. Whichever way you use them, I pray that the Holy Spirit will enrich your life through them.
**

Raphael Sunday Awoseyin
Founder and Author
Lagos, Nigeria

About the Author

Raphael Sunday Awoseyin is a Nigerian-born professional engineer, chartered in both Nigeria and the United Kingdom. As a boy, he was a devout Roman Catholic and served mass in the Catholic Church in his hometown. He came to a personal knowledge of Jesus Christ while in high school just before his 15th birthday in 1968. He has over 40 years of experience in the oil and gas industry and is also a keen software developer. He is a gifted Bible teacher, emphasizing the practical application of the Bible in the Christian's daily life. He is founder of the Danite companies Danite LLC and Danite Limited - a technology consulting group. His choice of the "Danite" brand for his Christian writings is to emphasise that, for a Christian, faith in Jesus Christ must shine through the vocational life. He is married to Sarah and they have three children – Yekemi, Adenike and Raphael (Jr) who are now all adults. You can send him a personal email at rsawoseyin@gmail.com.

About the Publisher – Otakada.org

About Otakada.org – We bring You Over 2,000,000 Faith-based and Faith Inspired Wholesome Products and Services For The Faith-Based Community And Online Seekers All In One Place!

Our Passion on otakada.org is to equip faith-based communities and to reach online seekers through wholesome content, products, and services that enhance holistically the spirit, the soul, and the body of the individual all in one place!

Who We are at Otakada.org is tied to our values, vision, and mission as highlighted hereunder:

Otakada Values: Integrity, Excellence, Speed, and profitability.

Otakada Vision: We envision a discipled world.

Otakada Mission: Our resources will be geared towards discovering, harnessing and liberating faith-based wholesome products and services for worldwide distribution and application.

Our goal at otakada.org is to effectively engage 100 million online community by 2040...stay with us.

Also, Shop for goods and services, gifts and much more at https://shop.otakada.org

This Edition

What we usually title The Parable of the Sower could also be titled The Parable of the Seeds – and we prefer this title for the purpose of this study because we are focusing on the Word - the seed. It is implicit in the parable that there was no difference in the quality of seeds that fell into different places.

The only difference was in the reception of the seeds – what happened to what was heard. Our response to what we hear makes the difference between salvation and damnation. If you came to know Christ through a message preached to a gathering of people, it is most probable that there were people in the same gathering who needed to be saved but who did not respond to the Gospel the way you did. Why did you respond and they did not? Read Hebrews 4:2 and Ephesians 2:8-9.

Enjoy!

**

Raphael Awoseyin
Lagos, Nigeria

Study 1 - Consider What You Hear!

Main Text: Mark 4:1-29

Key Verse: Mark 4:24 – "Consider carefully what you hear ... With the measure you use, it will be measured to you-- and even more." (NIV)
***

Our key verse warns us to carefully consider what we hear. We often quote this verse in the context of heeding the Gospel and coming to know Christ. But in fact, Jesus said those words to His disciples and not to the crowd (see v10). What did Jesus mean by the (NIV) statement "With the measure you use, it will be measured to you – and even more"? Many translations render this statement to mean that the measure you serve other people is the measure you will receive. While that may be true, the original rendition of this verse means something different. The statement, in the literal translation, reads: "... In what measure ye measure, it shall be measured to you; and to you who hear it shall be added." Note the words "to you who hear it shall be added". There is something about using what we hear that brings even more understanding of God's Word. The more we use what we hear, the more we hear from Him. Does this tell us something about situations when we wish God would speak to us about something and He seems silent?

Without doubt, one of the struggles Christians face today is the fact that much of what is heard and taught from the pulpits and various fellowships are not experienced by individuals, or even by the churches. We often say it is because we don't pray enough. We can ask the rhetorical question: "How much praying is enough?" But God constantly asks us what we are doing about what we hear. When was the last time you deliberately acted on something you learnt from the Bible (either from a preaching, teaching, or personal study) in such a way that it made you take a definite action, or brought about a definite change in you, your circumstance, or your relationships?

Discussion Questions:

1. "For this people's heart has become calloused; they hardly hear with their ears, and they have closed their eyes. Otherwise they might see with their eyes, hear with their ears, understand with their hearts and turn, and I would heal them." (Matthew 13:15 NIV). Describe what Jesus meant by a "calloused" heart.
2. Is it possible for a Christian's heart to be calloused? Give examples of indications of a calloused heart.

Key Learning Points:

1. We only get the benefit of what we hear when we act on it
2. Responding to the Gospel message to get saved requires God's grace
3. When we act on what God tells us, we open the door for Him to tell us more
4. When we repeatedly fail to act on what He tells us, our hearts could become calloused - no longer sensitive to His word, and we could wonder why He no longer speaks to us

5. A calloused heart could result from blindly holding on to denominational doctrines which may be unbiblical
6. A church can become calloused by holding on to norms and policies that are unbiblical

Prayer:

Father, open my heart to see how the things you reveal by your Spirit apply to me. Make me uneasy until I act on truths you reveal to me. In Jesus' name, Amen.

Study 2 - Nicodemus

Main Texts: John 3:1-15; 19:38-42

Key Verse: John 3:3 – Jesus replied, "Very truly I tell you, no one can see the kingdom of God unless they are born again." (NIV)
***

It is not explicitly recorded that Nicodemus had listened to Jesus Christ preach somewhere before that his historic night visit to Jesus, recorded in John 3. However, John recorded certain key events before the visit. These were that (a) John The Baptist had preached repentance and heralded Jesus' coming (John 1:15-27), (b) Jesus had been baptised (John 1:28-34), (c) Jesus had called his disciples (John 1:35-51), (c) Jesus had turned water into wine at Cana (John 2:1-11), and (d) Jesus had driven traders out of the temple courts (John 2:12-25). It seems likely that Nicodemus was among the Jews that took Jesus to task when Jesus drove the traders out of the temple. What he had seen and heard made such an impression on him that he decided to do something about it – go to Jesus secretly to find out what these things should mean for him, personally. The things God allows us to witness and hear are part of His message to us.

Have you ever been gripped by observations and words spoken, not necessarily targeting you, to the point of resolving to take an important personal decision?

Nicodemus was not only a Pharisee, he was also "a member of the Jewish ruling council". Imagine the personal struggles he would have been through before taking the step to go and speak with Jesus. This Jesus had a running battle with these Jewish leaders throughout His earthly ministry, culminating in His being handed over to be crucified. Considering that Nicodemus eventually joined in taking care of Jesus' body afterwards (John 19:38-42), he certainly remained a disciple. We do not know what his discipleship did to his standing as a Pharisee and as a member of the Jewish ruling council, but it is fair to suggest that he faced personal challenges as a result of his decision. Read John 7:40-53.

What thoughts of personal challenges could keep us from acting on what God tells us and how might we possibly resolve the inner conflicts?

The response of Jesus Christ to Nicodemus' inquiry was not the easiest to understand – not even for a well-learned Pharisee: "You must be born again". "You must be born of water and of the Spirit". One of the reasons many reject the Gospel today is that they think it does not make sense: How can God have a Son? How can the death of one man atone for the sins of the whole world? In helping Nicodemus understand, Jesus compared the working of the Holy Spirit to the way the wind blows: "The wind blows wherever it pleases. You hear its sound, but you cannot tell where it comes from or where it is going. So it is with everyone born of the Spirit." (John 3:8 NIV)

What role does our intellect play in our response, or lack of it, to God's word?

Discussion Questions:

1. In your local Church, it is possible that there are some who listen to messages and teachings but have never taken a step to receive Christ. What are the possible reasons?
2. Nicodemus did not quit the Jewish ruling council despite his apparent secret faith in Jesus Christ. What were his options and why did he remain in the council?

Key Learning Points:

1. Although Jesus was teaching and preaching in public places, the Holy Spirit targeted Nicodemus, leading him to respond to what he heard by seeking better understanding
2. The Holy Spirit is able to circumvent our intellect and enable us to have saving faith in Christ. Indeed, this has to happen especially with intellectuals
3. Nicodemus risked his reputation and standing in the society by seeking Jesus Christ, and eventually becoming His disciple
4. Despite his commitment to Jesus Christ, he chose not to leave the Jewish Council but rather remained as a voice for the Gospel. He remained a disciple and later publicly identified with Jesus by being directly involved in Jesus' burial

Responding positively to God's word could cost us our reputation, assets, and even our lives, but it is always the right thing to do

Prayer:

Father, grant me the courage and resolve to act on whatever I hear You speak to me, either directly or by observation of happenings around me. In Jesus' name, Amen.

Study 3 - Admirers and Agreers

Main Texts: Mark 12:18-34; Luke 11:14-28

Key Verse: Luke 11:28 - "Blessed rather are those who hear the word of God and obey it." (NIV)
***

The Sadducees who did not believe in the resurrection had engaged Jesus Christ in an intellectual debate with the primary objective of proving to Jesus that the idea of the resurrection did not make sense. Jesus made them see the shallowness of their reasoning. An unnamed Scribe who had listened to the conversation was pleased with Jesus' answer to the Sadducees. (Scribes believed in the resurrection.) Feeling good and perhaps wanting to feel confident about his standing with God, asked the question about which was most important commandment. Jesus summed all up the commandments into two simple commandments – love for God, and love for other people. The Scribe's response showed that he had the right intellectual understanding of the Scripture.

What did Jesus mean by "You are not far from the kingdom of God"? (Mark 12:34, NIV). Are you currently in this man's situation, or was there a time you were in his situation?

In our second text (Luke 11), a crowd had witnessed Jesus cast out a dumb demon. We see three different reactions from the crowd. One group was simply amazed and perhaps full of admiration for Jesus. A second group, unable to deny what they had seen, chose to ascribe what they saw to the devil. A third group was simply insatiable – they wanted to see even more miracles but were not prepared to believe in Him. From the first group ("The Admirers"), a woman shouted, "Blessed is the woman who gave you birth and nursed you!" to which Jesus replied, "Blessed are those who hear the word of God and obey it". (Luke 11:27-28).

Many institutional leaders, including heads of governments often commend their audience to the person of Jesus Christ as a "good example" to follow. What do you think is the value of such adulations to the cause of the Gospel?

There are today varied responses to God's word which may be good, but which do not necessarily benefit the respondent. Commending or congratulating a preacher for a "powerful" message is inadequate. Even agreeing with what the preacher says, or what we read in the Bible, is inadequate. When God said through prophet Isaiah that His word would accomplish what He sent it to accomplish (Isaiah 55:11), He did not mean any of these responses – He meant that things would happen in the lives of people, and in in the world, as a result of His word.

Mention some statements of Scripture which most Christians agree with but which may not necessarily be true in the life of the Christian.

Discussion Questions:

1.   What challenges does Christian evangelism face in a society where there seems to be pervasive intellectual understanding of the Gospel message, and how can Christians handle these in evangelism?
2.   Why do many people admire Jesus Christ but are not prepared to believe in Him with a view to being like Him?
***

Key Learning Points:

1.   Mental agreement, and even commendation of the words of Jesus Christ do not amount to salvation.
2.   Commendation by public dignitaries of Jesus Christ especially during Christian festive periods have little value to the salvation of the people
3.   Taking the definite step of making a personal commitment to Christ and the Scriptures is the only way to benefit from His word

Prayer:

Father, highlight to me aspects of my life and experience that do not align with what you say to me or about me. Grant me the grace to be the person you meant me to be. In Jesus' name, Ament.

Study 4 - Jairus

Main Texts: Mark 5:21-43

Key Verse: Mark 5:36 - "... Jesus told him, "Don't be afraid; just believe." (Mark 5:36 NIV)
***

The man Jairus was a synagogue leader and would be expected to uphold the official position of the synagogue leadership in all matters of faith and doctrine. This included repudiation of the claims of Jesus Christ. But Jairus had observed Jesus and listened to him. He had apparently witnessed how Jesus delivered the man with a legion of demons. He had listened to Jesus preach, and what he heard struck a chord in him – that Jesus must be capable of healing his sick daughter. He related what he had seen and heard from Jesus to his personal situation.

Have you ever been in a situation where evidences before you convinced you that the collective position of a group (or even a church) to which you belonged could be wrong and you were tempted to act contrary to the collective position?

Jairus summoned courage and pleaded with Jesus: "My little daughter is dying. Please come and put your hands on her so that she will be healed and live." (Mark 5:23 NIV). Jesus obliged and started to follow him to his house. But then Jesus got distracted by a woman who had touched his garment and received her healing. While He was attending to this woman, news came that Jairus' daughter had died. The three synoptic Gospels (Matthew,

Mark and Luke) record this story. Matthew records that on hearing this, Jairus said to Jesus: "My daughter has just died. But come and put your hand on her, and she will live." (Matthew 9:18). Jesus eventually got to Jairus' house and raised the girl back to life.

Why is it that those who were strongly antagonistic to the Gospel but become born again, tend to exhibit exceptional faith in God's word? What does this tell us about sharing the Gospel with unbelievers?

It is innate in us to expect God to address our situation in a certain way, and within a time frame we deem critical. Few of us would still retain hope after a loved one whose healing we have been praying for eventually dies. Jairus expected that Jesus would heal his daughter while she was still alive, but it did not work out that way.

What informs our expectation of how God would intervene in our situation, and our definition of a "critical time frame" for such intervention, and how might God respond to our expectation?

When Jesus delayed to the point of that the girl died, people told Jairus "Your daughter is dead … why bother the teacher anymore?" (Mark 5:35 NIV).

How do we manage the voices around us – especially of those we respect - that may be discouraging our taking God at His word?

Questions

1. Jairus apparently broke ranks with the synagogue leaders by acknowledging Jesus Christ and seeking Jesus' intervention in his family. Discuss why one might want to break ranks with his or her church's denominational beliefs.

2. Why do faithful Christians, despite confessions of faith and claims to what they understand to be God's promises, still sometimes face the embarrassment of not receiving what they desire from God?

***

Key Learning Points:

1. Those who are strongly antagonistic to the Gospel but who then come to know Christ tend to exercise greater faith in their Christian lives. This should encourage us to not give up in sharing the Gospel with strong antagonists

2. It is a bondage when we see that God's word challenges our long-held beliefs (perhaps from our denominational background) but we refuse to give up our erroneous traditional beliefs. Jairus allowed his personal conviction regarding Jesus to override the official Jewish leadership position.

3. We need to remind ourselves that God's workings are not constrained by our view of a "critical time frame" - that He is never too late in what He does.

Prayer:

Father, help me walk with you more closely so that as you revealed your ways to Moses, I will also know your ways and exercise faith in that knowledge. In Jesus' name, Amen

Study 5 - The centurion's servant

Main Text: Luke 7:1-10, Matthew 8:5-13

Key Verse: Matthew 8:8b - " ... just say the word, and my servant will be healed." (NIV)
***

A centurion in the Roman army was a commander of between 80 and 200 men. Several centurions feature in the New Testament. The first recorded conversion of a Gentile to the Christian faith was of the centurion in Caesarea (Acts 10). As with all military personnel of all ages, the centurion is very conscious of hierarchy and respects authority. In our main text for today, we have this centurion who, having heard of Jesus, came to the conclusion that Jesus must be capable of healing his servant who was ill. However, unlike the woman with haemorrhage who simply squeezed herself through the crowd to reach Jesus and touch his garment (Mark 5:25-34), this centurion believed he had to go through an intermediary to make his case to Jesus Christ. He reckoned that going through Jewish leaders would do it, since Jesus was of Jewish descent. So he approached the Jewish leaders to help plead his case. These leaders presented to Jesus what they considered to be a justification for helping the man: "This man deserves to have you do this, because he loves our nation and has built our synagogue." (Luke 7:4-5 NIV)

a) What motivates us, and what is our expectation when we approach a respected Christian leader to pray for us concerning an issue?

b) What unspoken but erroneous reasoning could underlie such request for prayer, and what are the potential consequences?

As Jesus accompanied the Jewish delegation to the centurion's house, the centurion on sighting them again sent friends to tell Jesus he didn't need to physically come to his house to effect the healing, but only needed to pronounce healing on his servant – from anywhere! (Matthew 8:8.) He hinged his submission on two counts: First, he deemed himself unworthy of Jesus' visit to his house. Secondly, he deemed such visit unnecessary anyway, and compared a word of Jesus to the word of a military commander who only needed to give orders and the troops obeyed. So, all these emissaries he was sending was just to get the word of healing from Jesus for his servant! After commending his unprecedented faith, Jesus indeed spoke the word of healing and the centurion's servant was healed immediately.

c) What do today's Christians need to be able to assert the centurion's kind of faith in the word of Jesus Christ concerning dire situations, and why do we often fail and face embarrassment when we make such faith declarations?

Discussion Questions:

1. Do you feel that some of the things we do like fasting and giving special offerings ("seed faith") when in a dire situation could be rooted in a thought of trying to

earn answers to our prayers? How do we guard against such motive?

2. How does Jesus speak to situations today in such a way that we can also go away with full assurance that it is done?

***

Key Learning Points:

1. When we request prayer support from a respected Christian concerning an issue, we should not do so as if he or she has better access to God. The intent should be: (a) Possible counsel concerning the issue, to help us pray more effectively, and (b) In obedience to the Scripture admonition for us to pray for one another

2. We must guard against ascribing answers to our prayers to some "man of God" as that would amount to sharing God's glory with man. Indeed, such a mindset could hinder answers to our prayers

3. Our ability to assert the Centurion's kind of faith ("Just speak the word, and my servant will be healed") can only come from a close walk with God, meditation on His word, speaking those words to ourselves, and making them our own.

Prayer:

Father, thank you for making me worthy to come to you, for any situation I face through none other but your Son Jesus Christ. Help me discern and trust you when you speak to my situations. In Jesus' name, Amen.

Study 6 - Levels of Faith

Main Text: Mark 5:22-43, Matthew 8:5-13

Key Verse: Matthew 9:29 - " ... Then he touched their eyes and said, 'According to your faith let it be done to you.'" (NIV)

***

In this study, we compare three persons each of whom responded positively, in faith, to the word of Jesus Christ. In our first text, we see two of these characters: Jairus' daughter was ill and he desperately wanted Jesus to come to his house to heal her. To Jairus, the answer lay in Jesus' physical presence at the girl's bedside. Then we have the woman that had been bleeding for twelve years. The words and works of Jesus inspired her faith and she said to herself, "If I just touch his clothes, I will be healed." (Mark 5:28 NIV). One might be surprised that she did not seek for Jesus to pray for her or lay hands on her! Then in our second text, we see the third character - the centurion who was satisfied that all he needed for his servant's healing was a word from Jesus, spoken from anywhere!

a)   Give examples of different levels of faith expressed by people seeking God's intervention in their situation today.

b)   What should be the attitude of other Christians around them, some of whom may in fact feel uncomfortable or awkward with the seeker's demonstration of faith?

The woman with haemorrhage had significant challenges. First was the fact that at that time, women were not expected to openly mingle with men in public places. (This explains why, for example, the account of Jesus feeding thousands miraculously only refers to men, "besides women and children".) Furthermore, according to the law, a haemorrhaging woman was unclean and should not mingle with healthy people. See Leviticus 15:25-27. These challenges were definitely sufficient for her to resign herself to her fate. But she had a faith that rose above those challenges.

c)   Give examples of real challenges we could face as we seek God's intervention in our situation, and possible lessons from this woman's story on our response to such challenges.

The idea of a woman touching Jesus' garment to be healed, which was somewhat mirrored in Apostle Paul's ministry at Ephesus where handkerchiefs and aprons from his body were taken to the sick for healing (Acts 19:11-12) has informed the practice of "holy handkerchiefs", "holy water", "holy oil", etc. in Churches today.

d)   What are the subtle dangers in the use of "holy" articles taken from respected ministers as a means of solving our life's problems?

e)   What would be a scripturally balanced attitude to such practice?

***

Key Learning Points:

1.   The three characters Jairus, the bleeding woman, and the centurion with a sick servant, all exercised different levels of faith but the Lord honoured them all
2.   We should respect individuals' exercise of faith even if it makes us feel awkward
3.   As we exercise faith in taking God at His word, there will always be challenges which could be from the reality on the ground or people around us who may either tell us our case is beyond prayer, or that we are responsible for our predicament as so should not seek relief
4.   We must hold on to God's word and not be deterred by the challenges
5.   Objects like handkerchiefs, anointing oil, holy water, etc. may help the faith of some people as "contact objects" but we must never see these objects as having any power as all healing comes from our trust in God through Jesus Christ.

Prayer:

Father, as I study your word, let your revelations to me become a part of me, manifesting in my increasing levels of faith and trust in you. In Jesus' name, Amen

Study 7 - The Pentecost Crowd

Main Text: Acts 2:1-41

Key Verse: Acts 2:37 - " When the people heard this, they were cut to the heart and said to Peter and the other apostles, 'Brothers, what shall we do?'" (NIV)"

***

The New Testament event we call Pentecost started with about 120 disciples gathered in a room, praying - Acts 1:14-15. Then there was seemed to be a bizarre event – a mighty rushing wind, tongues that looked like fire, people speaking in languages they had never learnt which however were understood by outsiders who were not part of the "madness". The reactions were not unexpected: "What does this mean?" "They are drunk". In case someone thought this was a one-off event, something similar happened much later in the home of Cornelius – Acts 10:44-45. Did the Holy Spirit who was behind all these realise how "bizarre" this whole thing was?

a)   What are our honest feelings – spoken and unspoken – when we witness what seems to be a disruption of our orderly fellowship by what people ascribe to the Holy Spirit?

Peter, flanked by the other apostles, seeing the bewilderment of the onlookers stood up to explain the strange phenomenon in the light of the Scriptures. Hear how he started: "These people are not drunk, as you suppose. It's only nine in the morning! No, this is what was spoken by the prophet Joel ..." (Acts 2:15-16 NIV). He continued, drawing the attention of the people to the Scriptural explanation for what seemed bizarre.

b) What is the role of the Church leadership in the supernatural manifestations of the Holy Spirit in the congregation and how is he prepared for this role?

c) What do you think would have happened if Peter and the other Apostles had simply ignored the remarks and carried on with the prayer meeting?

Peter's message was powerful, prompting these onlookers to ask "What shall we do?" (v37). The people accepted that what they had just heard called for a definite response on their part. But they did not know what that response should be, and they wanted Peter to tell them. Peter's response was clear and concise: Repent and get baptized in the name of Jesus Christ so your sins can be forgiven and you will receive the gift of the Holy Spirit. This forgiveness of sins and the gift of the Holy Spirit are available to you, your children, other nationalities and even to those unborn. Don't let the corrupted society around you determine your destiny! (v38).

d) Let each participant write down in 2 minutes "a 10-second Gospel message" and 3 people share theirs with the group.

We are told that about 3,000 people who accepted his message were baptized (v41). It is implied that not everyone who heard the message accepted it.

e) What are the possible responses – spoken or unspoken - from individuals after listening to a Bible-based message?

***

Key Learning Points:

1. Some of us may feel awkward at manifestations of the Holy Spirit in our congregation, but we should accept that the Holy Spirit manifests as He pleases

2.   The Church leadership has a responsibility to moderate manifestations to avoid disorderliness and ensure the Church truly benefits from ministrations of the Holy Spirit

3.   The Church leadership also needs to always explain the Scriptural context of manifestations of the Holy Spirit, for the benefit of the congregation. (This would be similar to the way the Holy Communion is always explained in Scriptural context.)

4.   We need to have a clear understanding of what the core Gospel message is: It is about salvation through faith in Jesus Christ whom God gave to die for our sins. While we find solutions to life's challenges such as health and material needs in Christ, this should not be seen as "The Gospel".

Prayer:

Father, open my heart to your messages that I hear or read in your word so that I always respond in the way you expect. In Jesus' name, Amen.

Study 8 – Apostle Paul

Main Text: Galatians 2:11-24; 2 Corinthians 11:23-33

Key Verse: Galatians 1:11-12 - " I want you to know ... that the gospel I preached is not of human origin. I did not receive it from any man, nor was I taught it; rather, I received it by revelation from Jesus Christ." (NIV) "
***

Apostle Paul, in defending the authenticity of his ministry, tells the Galatians about the early days of his conversion. Specifically, he says the Lord Jesus Christ revealed the Gospel to him directly, that it was not something he learnt from the apostles before him. The details of that revelation are not recorded in the Bible, but we do know that when the Lord visited the disciple Ananias in Damascus and told him to go see Saul (as Paul was called then), the Lord said concerning Saul: "This man is my chosen instrument to proclaim my name to the Gentiles and their kings and to the people of Israel. I will show him how much he must suffer for my name." (Acts 9:15-16 NIV). In fact, he says when he received the revelation of the Gospel, he did not even consult those earlier apostles (Peter, James, John, etc.) for any form of clarification or authentication (see vv15-17).

a) In your opinion, why did Paul choose not to consult those who were apostles before him concerning God's revelation to him?

b)   Are there revelations to individual Christians today that may not be appropriate to "clarify" or "validate" with older, perhaps more mature Christians?

The Lord had told Ananias concerning Saul, "... I will show him how much he must suffer for my name." This must have been part of the revelation Paul received from the Lord which he did not discuss with anyone. In our second text, Paul catalogues his sufferings in the course of preaching the Gospel. We later read (See Acts 21:10-14) of how God through Agabus revealed that Apostle Paul would be arrested and maltreated in Jerusalem.

c)   Why might God reveal to an individual impending sufferings, hardships or calamities?

d)   What are our typical responses to such revelations when they concern us or someone we care about?

When a Christian undergoes suffering which could reasonably have been foreseen or which had previously been revealed would come, there is often a feeling of regret that perhaps we should have acted differently to avert the suffering.

e)   What practical steps can the suffering Christian take when faced with the thought that the suffering could have been averted had he or she acted differently?

f)   How can other Christians support such a suffering Christian, particularly in managing the feeling of regret?

There are revelations that are meant for our action only. When we follow God's directives and we suffer in the process, we should remember that the early apostles had the same experience!

***

Key Learning Points:

1. There are God's revelations to us as individuals which He expects us to act upon and not discuss with even those we respect.
2. The fact that we are acting in obedience to God's revelation does not mean that the road will be smooth all through. Despite Paul's obedience, he had a hard time throughout his ministry
3. God's revelations to us of impending suffering may not always be with a view for us to pray that God should disallow the suffering. It may be to prepare us to go through it.

Prayer:

Father, teach me to handle your revelations to me as you intend, and grant me the grace to accept whatever comes my way in the course of such obedience, Amen

Study 9 - Thessalonians and Bereans

Main Text: Acts 17:1-15

Key Verse: Acts 17:11 – "Now the Berean Jews were of more noble character than those in Thessalonica, for they received the message with great eagerness and examined the Scriptures every day to see if what Paul said was true." (NIV)

***

Apostle Paul was the one apostle specifically mandated to take the Gospel to the non-Jewish world –see Acts 9:15. His missionary journeys targeted Gentile routes, but the Gentile cities he visited also had sizeable Jewish populations. He adopted a multi-pronged approach to his Gospel outreach: He combined marketplace evangelistic outreaches – which mostly targeted the Gentiles, with synagogue-based Scripture discourses which targeted Jews and Proselytes (Gentile converts to Judaism). See Acts 17:1-3, 6-17.

a) Is there a need to tailor our evangelistic outreach style to particular mind sets? If so, what would be the key differences in approach between reaching out to Muslims, nominal Christians, and traditionalists?

Our key verse makes an unusual comparison between the Jews in Thessalonica and those in Berea. It uses the term "more noble character" to describe the Bereans, for the simple reason that they did not only received the message "with great eagerness", they also "examined the Scriptures every day to see if what Paul said was true".

One of the challenges respected Christian leaders face today is that many of their hearers accept and even quote what they teach, hardly establishing the Bible basis for the teachings.

b)	What are the dangers of holding on to specific teachings (even when such teachings are beneficial) because we heard them from respected leaders, without establishing the Scriptural basis?

c)	How can Bible preachers and teachers help their hearers establish the basis of what they belief in the Scriptures rather than in their own (preacher's/teacher's) respectability?

Just as one could erroneously hold on to, and live by teachings of individual respectable Christian leaders, it is also possible to hold on to teachings on purely denominational grounds. Actually, if all church teachings were stripped of all denomination-specific teachings, what would be left would be the pure Scripture which binds all Christians all over the world together. While many denominational teachings are sound and have a good basis, it is important that we recognise them as denomination-specific and should therefore not hinder fellowship with other Christians. Read 1 Corinthians 7:12.

d)	How can we identify teachings that are based on denominational judgement rather than Scripture injunction, especially as we do not often hear the type of qualification Paul gave in 1 Corinthians 7:12 with what our denominations teach or preach?

e)	Mention some denomination-specific teachings, either in your church or other churches you know, that are based on denominational judgment rather than direct Scriptural injunction. What is the appropriate way to disseminate such teachings?

***

Key Learning Points:

1. Just as Paul adopted a multi-pronged approach to sharing the Gospel with the diverse populations, we need to also adopt appropriate strategies as we share the Gospel with Muslims, nominal Christians and other unbelievers. The same approach may not work for every group.
2. It is important that our core faith and beliefs are based on God's word and not what some respected Christian leaders tell us, or even our denomination's specific teachings. When a brother or sister points out a Scripture truth us, we should not thenceforth ascribe the truth to the brother or the sister; it is God's word.
3. Denomination-specific teachings which are well intentioned are good, but we should not present them as being Scripture teachings or at the same level with the Scriptures. If we avoid this pitfall, we would see far fewer reasons for acrimony between denominations

Prayer:

Father, I commit to studying your word to know what it says so that my faith will be based on what You say and not on man's view. Help me to apply the Scripture test to all I hear, in Jesus' name. Amen.

Study 10 - The Ephesians

Main Text: Acts 19:1-41

Key Verse: Acts 19:17 – "When this became known to the Jews and Greeks living in Ephesus, they were all seized with fear, and the name of the Lord Jesus was held in high honour." (NIV)
***

Paul and Silas stayed quite a while at Ephesus, preaching the Gospel in public places and holding discourses with Jews in the synagogues. Throughout this period, God honoured His word and wrought many miracles through the apostles. Initially, many who believed, afraid of what other people would think of them, kept their faith secret. But it got to a point they could not keep it secret any longer – they openly declared their faith in Christ and brought out all articles of their idolatry to be destroyed – Acts 19:18-20. Our key verse says the people "were all seized with fear".

a) What different kinds of fear could arise in those exposed to the preaching of God's word under the anointing of the Holy Spirit?

There is a fear that leads to repentance and salvation. This was the kind of fear that made those bystanders on the day of Pentecost ask, "What shall we do?" – Acts 2:37. It was this same kind of fear that led the Ephesians to renounce idolatry and embrace the Gospel. However, a silversmith by name Demetrius had a different kind of fear.

b)   What was Demetrius' basic fear and what other fears did he spin from this basic fear with a view to mobilising support for his opposition to the Gospel?

c)   What fears today keep people from responding positively to the Gospel message, and how are these fears often played up to win public support for opposition to the Gospel?

Ephesus was a Gentile city, and here were Paul and Silas – Jewish preachers, preaching what the Gentiles saw as undermining the supremacy of Artemis, the god of the people. It seems the Jews felt obliged to protect the apostles and defuse the tension. So they got Alexander – a Jew – to try to calm the frayed nerves of the protesters. (See vv33-34.) He got on stage but the crowd would not let him speak because they knew him to be a Jew. It was the city clerk who eventually took the stage and calmed the people by reaffirming the supremacy of Artemis – the Ephesian god – and instigating a spontaneous praise of this god. Paul later made reference to this same Alexander in his letters to Timothy: Read 1 Timothy 1:18-20 and 2 Timothy 4:14.

d)   From later references to Alexander the silversmith (also called "the coppersmith", what qualities did the Jews see in him that made him a candidate to pacify the riotous crowd?

e)   Are there characters in the Church today that could play a similar role to what Alexander was to play in event of attacks on the Church?

While we love the Scriptures that promise us good things and encourage us, God's word would also inspire fear in us, and this is appropriate. What we do in response to that fear determines our destiny. God intends the fear to lead us to repentance. But if we embolden ourselves and

suppress the fear, we could over time develop a calloused spirit that God's word may no longer be able to penetrate.
***

Key Learning Points:

1. Many are hindered from receiving the baptism in the Holy Spirit by fear of unusual things they might experience, such as speaking in tongues - Thwy want the Holy Spirit but do not want to give Him the freedom to act in their lives
2. Fear is an appropriate response to God's word
3. The fear we experience from reading or hearing God's word should make us align our lives to His purposes
4. It is dangerous to suppress the fear brought about by God's word with a view to "feeling good". If we continue to resist His word, we could over time develop a calloused spirit that is no longer sensitive to Him

Prayer:

Father, when your word pierces my heart and makes me uncomfortable, please help me take the right step to align with you. Never allow me be comfortable in resisting your word. In Jesus' name. Amen

Study 11 – Governor Felix

Main Text: Acts 24:1-27

Key Verse: Acts 24:25 – " As Paul talked about righteousness, self-control and the judgment to come, Felix was afraid and said, "That's enough for now! You may leave. When I find it convenient, I will send for you." (NIV)

In Acts 21:10-14 we had read of Agabus prophesying that Paul would be arrested and bound in Jerusalem, and would be handed over to the Gentiles. The other disciples had tried fruitlessly to dissuade Paul from going to Jerusalem, to avoid this unpleasant experience. But Paul's response was "I am ready not only to be bound, but to die in Jerusalem for the name of Jesus". In our text for today, we see that prophecy come to pass as Jews from Asia stirred up hostility against Paul in Jerusalem and he was eventually handed over by the religious leaders to the Gentiles.

a)   Can you recall a prophecy or prevailing circumstances pointing to a risk of severe suffering for a Christian but he or she still chose to face it?

b)   What is the attitude of Christians to other Christians caught in severe suffering where such suffering had been reasonably foreseen or even foretold through some revelation? What should be our attitude?

Paul eventually appeared before Governor Felix at Caesarea. We are told (v22) that even before Paul's appearance before him, Felix "was well acquainted with the Way" – he knew about the Christians and the Gospel message. On Paul's second appearance before him – this time with Felix's wife in attendance, we are told: "As Paul talked about righteousness, self-control and the judgment to come, Felix was afraid and said, 'That's enough for now! You may leave. When I find it convenient, I will send for you.'" (v25).

c)   How do we recognise those that are "well acquainted with the Way" but are not born again, and what should be the Christian's approach to evangelism towards such people?

d)   Why would someone hear the Gospel message, be afraid, and yet not take the necessary step to be saved? Over a period of two years, Felix left Paul in prison, calling for him frequently in the hope that Paul would give him a bribe to be released – vv26-27. There are probably some people languishing in our prisons today on trumped-up charges and for no offence other than that they would not give a bribe. The Christian would be under pressure to secure the release of such people in the shortest possible time. Many of us get into "small prisons" from time to time – like when a corrupt official holds us to ransom to force a bribe before we can get justice.

e)   What practical actions can a local church take on account of people known to be unjustly imprisoned?

f)   Would you help raise funds to give to government officials for the release of a loved one who is being unjustly held in prison?.

***

Key Learning Points:

1.   God could reveal impending suffering to His children, not so they would pray against it, but that they

should be prepared to face it; He does not always prevent suffering even when we pray against it

2. It is particularly challenging to minister the Gospel to those who are already acquainted with it but have not yielded their lives to Christ because they fear the consequence on their earthly status

3. We will sometimes face unjust suffering and be pressured to compromise our faith and integrity to secure our freedom. We need wisdom and the fortitude of The Holy Spirit to remain aligned to God in such situations

Prayer:

Father, we pray for those in our midst who may be well acquainted with the Gospel but have not received you as Lord and Saviour, that your word may come alive in their hearts and lead them to salvation. In Jesus' name. Amen

Study 12 - Festus and Agrippa

Main Texts: Acts 26:1-32

Key Verse: Acts 26:20b – " ... Stop sinning and turn to God! Then prove what you have done by the way you live." (NIV)

***

Governor Felix had handed over Apostle Paul as a prisoner, to his successor Festus. On Festus' maiden visit to Jerusalem, the Jews and their religious leaders had again demanded for Paul be sent back to Jerusalem – ostensibly to face charges, but in reality, with a view to ambushing and killing him on his way - Acts 25:3. Festus declined sending Paul to Jerusalem but instead asked the accusers to come to Caesarea to present their case against Paul. Paul's accusers followed Festus to Caesarea and make their case. After listening to Paul's defence, Festus was not convinced that Paul had done any wrong. In the course of his defence, Paul requested to be sent to Emperor Caesar in Rome for trial. It was today's equivalent of appealing to the Supreme Court. However, in sending Paul to Rome, Festus would have to state Paul's alleged offence – which he did not believe existed. To help him in this regard, he called Paul to state his case before his (Festus') visiting King Agrippa.

a) Why do you think Paul appealed to Caesar – a process that would further prolong his case? Do you see any parallel between the circumstance that led to Paul's appeal and the situation in your country's judiciary today?

Acts 9:10-16 tells us what God told Ananias about Paul and his future ministry following conversion. Paul later in Galatians 1:15-16 made reference to what God told him in this regard. However, it was before King Agrippa (Acts 26:13-18) that he gave the detailed message he received from God concerning his ministry.

"It is hard for you to kick against the goads." – Acts 26:14b. The Good News translation renders it thus: "You are hurting yourself by hitting back, like an ox kicking against its owner's stick." Give examples today of how God's move is being obstructed in a manner that amounts to kicking "against the goads".

Paul's defence – or rather, sermon – before Agrippa (and Festus) shows Paul drawing from incontrovertible scriptural truths, to establish the Gospel message. The two dignitaries reacted differently to the message.

b)   What specific statement (see v23) of Paul prompted Festus to say he (Paul) was out of his mind and why?

c)   What elements of the Gospel make no sense to people like Festus today, and how do those who come to Christ deal with such issues in their minds to come to Christ?

d)   King Agrippa's remarked to Paul: "Do you think that in such a short time you can persuade me to be a Christian?". What do you think was going on in Agrippa's mind that prompted this remark and what does this say about many who hear the Gospel today?

We have no record that Agrippa eventually accepted the Gospel to which Paul brought him to understand. But the Christian's mandate in witnessing is to lead people to a point of understanding.

***

Key Learning Points:

1.   Obedience to God may well prolong our suffering as we may sometimes have to navigate a tortuous legal process, but we must continue to assure ourselves that God is in charge
2.   There will always be people to whom the Gospel makes no logical sense, and there will be those who see sense in it, are at the threshold of receiving it, but resist it nevertheless
3.   Our objective in sharing the Gospel is to lead people to understand God's plan of salvation. Only God's grace leads those who so understand to salvation.

Prayer:

Father, we pray for those we encounter who are struggling to make sense of the Gospel, that your grace may reach them to open the eyes of their understanding and receive your salvation. In Jesus' name. Amen.
End

www.ingramcontent.com/pod-product-compliance
Lightning Source LLC
LaVergne TN
LVHW021741060526
838200LV00052B/3410